IMMIGRATION CHARITY E-BOOK

THE INVALUABLE GUIDE

This is an invaluable guide for social entrepreneurs and non-profit religious, charitable, social service, or similar organizations. It is specifically written for those who wish to start and/or operate an immigration-law non-profit in USA.
This guide is devised by ExecVisa

Immigration Charity E-book

By

ExecVisa™

Published By
ExecVisa

Copyright © 2015

License Notes

Overview

The year 2015 has witnessed the biggest immigration crisis since the Second World War. More US based social entrepreneurs and non-profit religious, charitable, social service, or similar organizations are starting an immigration law program. However, many struggle to understand the process of starting this pro bono/free and/or low-cost, nominal fee, legal service.

ExecVisa is a team of experienced professionals and partners that advise and guide those with such aims. They have a network of carefully selected strategic partners plus close ties to accomplish the various tasks. They also guide students, graduates, businesses, entrepreneurs and investors, in identifying and seeking the most suitable form of visa to their needs. ExecVisa develop and compile all the necessary documents and reports required for submission to the US Citizenship & Immigration Services (USCIS). Most importantly, through monthly events in various countries, ExecVisa equip you with all that is demanded by USCIS' strict scrutiny. They are also the authors of the book "ExecVisa" which has been translated into a variety of languages. The book explains how you go about obtaining the many types of visa that allow you to work legally or do business in USA. It contains more than 100 pages filled with the knowhow you need to have at your fingertips.

Connect with ExecVisa

Website: www.execvisa.com

Like us on Facebook: www.facebook.com/execvisa

Smashwords Author Profile:
https://www.smashwords.com/profile/view/execvisa

Other books by ExecVisa are listed in the final pages of this book.

Open forum – you can make suggestions for the next ebook edition

If you are an immigration enthusiast/expert, and would

like to suggest additional topics to be covered in this ebook, please email them to us (team@execvisa.com) with your suggestions for inclusion. This current ebook edition is devised specifically for immigration charities in USA.

Additional countries

If you would like the next edition of the ebook to include chapters relevant to other countries please nominate your preferences.

Book Chapters:

1: Recognition and Accreditation explained

Accreditation (a) and (b)

It is a requirement that you achieve accreditation status, at least for your agency, and, perhaps, for some of your staff members. If your intention is to exercise both options, the submission is best done simultaneously. This will make the process simpler and faster in obtaining a decision. There are two levels of accreditation, *Partial* and *Full*.

Accreditation (a) Partial

In the case of *partial accreditation*, a representative is permitted to practice within the USCIS system. In so doing, they can assist their clients in a wide range of ways. These can include making written or oral submissions on the client's behalf to the USCIS; to an official (with or without the client being in attendance); signing documents on the client's behalf and such like. The strategy of first seeking, *only partial accreditation*, is the recommended option, in the absence of one being expert in the full gambit of Immigration Law.

Accreditation (b) Full

In order that a representative can practise in a more comprehensive manner before USCIS it is essential to acquire *full accreditation.* This permits the representative to make representations to the Executive Office for Immigration Review (EOIR). The Immigration Court and the BIA are embraced by the EOIR. When fully accredited, one can represent a client in dealings with both of these entities.

However, full accreditation does not bestow permission to a non-attorney to represent clients in any form of law court.

The benefits of Recognition and Accreditation

There are very many benefits that come with this process. Firstly, there are no costs involved, it is free. In addition, the procedure is uncomplicated, simple to understand and follow. Thousands of agencies just like yours have gone through the process and been granted both recognition and accreditation. You avoid any expensive legal fees because your trained staff can handle the needs of your clients. In so doing they are not acting as attorneys nor are they engaging in the practice of law.

Duration - caution

Once a representative has been accredited they can continue to work in this capacity provided they apply to renew their status every three years. In this regard, it is important to remember to make the application to renew at least 60 days before the accreditation expires. In this way valid accreditation will exist whilst awaiting the BIA's decision on the granting of the renewal.

Enhanced service

Having an accredited representative ensures that a client enjoys a number of wide ranging benefits. These include making enquiries on behalf of their client s and representing them at relevant hearings and interviews that may arise. The agency will be enabled to file such forms as a G-28 "Notice of Entry of Appearance" with applications. In so doing it puts the USCIS on notice that it is representing the client in question. This, in turn, ensures that USCIS will send a copy of all pertinent correspondence it sends to that client.

The disadvantages of Recognition and Accreditation

Each agency is permitted, by the BIA, to charge nominal fees to clients for the services it provides to clients. There are no strict guidelines as to what level of fees that can be charged. The BIA evaluates each agency's funding ability. It assesses whether or not the agency receives sufficient income, from the fees it derives from its clients, to support its work. If the agency can survive on these fees alone then the BIA will hardly view the fees as being nominal. Therefore, you should undertake some research elsewhere to establish what level of fee is acceptable to the BIA.

One office/location

When you receive approval from the BIA, it will be solely in respect of the office and location stipulated in your submission. If you have more than one office, and you seek approval for them, a separate application must be made in respect of each one. You may occasionally undertake some outreach work away from the granted office. Provided that the vast majority of the legal work involved takes place in the approved office it is unnecessary for that field work to apply for recognition.

One person, one office.

Once an operative is accredited, that status is fixed to the office in which the person is stationed. If that person moves to a different office a new application must be made seeking to have the person in question accredited to that office.

Multi office accreditation

If someone wants to work in more than one office, either in a full or part time capacity, each of those offices must have that person accredited to their particular office.

Certificates of Service on USCIS and Immigration and Customs Enforcement (ICE)

In the case where an *accreditation only* request is submitted, further requirements pertain. It is essential that your request be copied to the District Director and the Chief Council of ICE who control the area in which your agency is located. The submission should also include details of the BIA Certificate of Service, itemising how it was dispatched, by whom, and the date on which it was sent.

Applying for Accreditation Only - Samples

CERTIFICATE OF SERVICE

I, [Name of Person Mailing], hereby certify that on this [date] day of [month], [year], I mailed by U.S. mail a copy of the Application for Accreditation of Representative to the District Director for CIS:

[add address of CIS District Office]

By: _____[signature] [Name of Person Mailing]

CERTIFICATE OF SERVICE

I, [Name of Person Mailing], hereby certify that on this [date] day of [month], [year], I mailed by U.S. mail a copy of the Application for Accreditation of Representative to the local Chief Counsel for Immigration and Customs Enforcement (ICE) at:

[add address of ICE Chief Counsel Office]

By: _____[signature] [Name of Person Mailing]

2: How you go about - Recognition and Accreditation

First and foremost, to establish an immigration law program, recognition and accreditation must be obtained from the US Board of Immigration Appeals (BIA). The recognition of organizations and the accreditation of non-attorney representatives include many regulations. They govern the requirements and procedures for authorizing the representatives of non-profit entities. These include religious, charitable, social service, or similar organizations. They represent persons in proceedings before the Executive Office for Immigration Review (EOIR) and the Department of Homeland Security.

Currently, the US BIA does not give recognition to an agency that does not have at least a partially accredited representative with access to technical support. Heretofore, agencies that did not have immigration attorneys on their staff could apply for recognition. This was permitted at the outset provided they applied for the accreditation of their staff at a later time.

Major change

However, this is no longer possible. Agencies that are devoid of suitably qualified immigration attorneys on their staff need to submit their recognition and accreditation application at the same time. In the case where an agency's staff is only partially accredited, it is essential to show that technical support does exist when the application is submitted and provide written support for this assertion.

Proof required

In the event that you are an element within a national network, that has access to immigration attorneys, you must prove this claim by means of written confirmation from the attorney being sited. On the other hand, if such is not the case, you could seek the services of a local immigration attorney in a consultative capacity. This too requires substantive confirmation.

Corporate Social Responsibility

ExecVisa specializes in assisting social entrepreneurs, non-profit religious, charitable, social service, or similar organizations to start an immigration law program. One that has a robust recognition and accreditation. This is to ensure that these entities comply consistently with good Corporate Social Responsibility.

Meet the essential requirements

The following list is your simple to understand 20-point check-list for establishing an immigration law program and receiving recognition and accreditation from BIA.

- Download and complete the EOIR-31 form (Latest pdf Version available from Justice.Gov at http://www.justice.gov/sites/default/files/pages/attachments/2015/07/24/eoir31.pdf);

- You should mail your original request to BIA at:

> R&A Coordinator
>
> Board of Immigration Appeals
>
> Office of the Chief Clerk
>
> 5107 Leesburg Pike, Suite 2000
>
> Falls Church, VA 22041.

- Send one copy of each to the local USCIS District Director and ICE local Chief Counsel. Their addresses are found at:

> USCIS: http://www.uscis.gov/about-us/find-uscis-office/field-offices
>
> ICE: http://www.ice.gov/contact/legal

- For the purpose of BIA accreditation, provide Certificates of service on USCIS and ICE;

- Cover letter explaining what the agency does and why it merits recognition;

- Evidence of Tax-Exempt Status IRS 501(c)(3);

- By-Laws;

- Articles of Incorporation;

- Media/PR materials, Local newspaper articles showcasing agency's great work (optional);

- Provide a list of names on staff and supporters. Here is a useful list:

>Affiliate Director;
>
>Receptionist;
>
>Reception and Placement Director;
>
>Partial accredited representative (Immigration/Legal Department Supervisor and Attorney/BIA Rep);
>
>Case Manager (a);
>
>Case Manager (b);
>
>Immigration Case Worker;
>
>Legal Intern;
>
>Two referees (e.g. influential people such as a local Mayor, politician, philanthropist or advocate);
>
>One referee who will provide technical support to the partial accredited representative.

- You should submit an immigration Resume/CV pertaining to any member of staff who has obtained immigration training and/or experience. This can have taken the form of them providing technical assistance or being in a supervisory role as an immigration attorney or a fully accredited staff member. Their contribution may have been as a consultant, in a paid or unpaid, capacity.

Stipulate the period of time that was devoted to training. Provide supportive detail as to the name of the organisation that undertook the training; details of the subject matter covered; its duration; and if certification was awarded at its conclusion.

All of the above should be augmented by the submission of printed material such as training programmes, the titles of each immigration law training course, the names of attendees and the certificates awarded to each one;

- Business plan for the Immigration Legal Program (below are key sections to include in the plan);

> Organization profile;
>
> Market analysis;
>
> Market strategy;
>
> Services;
>
> Operations;
>
> Timeline;
>
> Policies and procedures manuals;
>
> Finances;
>
> Case mix;
>
> Conclusion.

- List of agency's immigration library resources;

- List of fees for immigration services (must be nominal);

- Brief list of agency's funding sources and budget showing income and expenses;

- Organizational chart, showing supervision of immigration staff;

- Caseload of staff;

- Two Letters of recommendation, usually from influential people, such as a local Mayor (for example), and not from an attorney or accredited representative;

- One Letter giving proof of technical support from an attorney;

- Any funding, grants or donations already raised for the new immigration legal program (optional).

3: The 10 Tips for a successful immigration-law charity

When you have achieved recognition and accreditation, here is a useful 10-point check list for running a successful immigration legal program:

- List of Immigration Case Management Systems;

- Non-Attorney Volunteer Agreement;

- Volunteer Confidentiality Agreement;

- Organisation's Policy Agreement: prohibition against providing legal services outside the office and expectations of employees;

- Case Notes Form for case file;

- Client Retainer Agreement;

- Client Intake Form;

- Media and Communications Memorandum: What to do and say when contacted by the media;

- Consent form for interviews by the media; and

- Brief list of guidelines for communication and public relations (PR).

Here to help you

Contact ExecVisa (team@execvisa.com) in respect of guidelines for the Board of Immigration Appeals (BIA) requirements. ExecVisa can also guide you with drafting a Business Plan for an immigration legal program.

Avail of experience and expertise

In order to assist them, and likeminded others, in this deserving cause and objective, ExecVisa mobilised its expertise and experience to provide guidance and advice. Apart from setting out all the essential steps, ExecVisa are on hand to answer queries for all entities on a plethora of issues from drafting business plans to fund raising activities.

Additional support

Further guidance can be had for grant writing and fund raising activities (as well as philanthropists/grant providers and strategy). In addition, ExecVisa provides further information on how to achieve additional recognition from the Council on Accreditation COA (an optional accreditation that adds more credibility to an Immigration Law program).

Multilingual

ExecVisa translates its work into the language of various nationalities, to ease understanding and implementation of our advice and guidelines. If your language has not yet been covered in our endeavours please email us (team@execvisa.com) and we will immediately begin the process. We are here to help you. Help us in this pursuit by keeping us informed of your needs.

4: The book "ExecVisa" is the "must have" book for you

In 2015, ExecVisa published the ExecVisa book on how you go about obtaining many types of visa that allow you to work or do business legally in USA. This invaluable guide book has been published in a variety of languages (in both print and ebook versions). The book is an easy to read and understand guide. It explains what's needed to secure a US visa to meet the immigrant's needs. If you are an immigrant, it tells you what you require to know and have for discussion with your immigration lawyer. This saves you a great amount of your time and your money. It cuts down on expensive legal fees and speeds up the process. The book is wide-ranging without being exhaustive.

Invaluable guidelines

It supplies you with invaluable guidelines and includes 8 ways to work or do business legally in USA and 6 ways to stay in USA permanently (Green Card eligibility - unfamiliar to you). Non-nationals have a keen interest in entrepreneurship/start-up in USA. To further assist them to achieve their aims we include in the book an extra bonus. It contains most helpful chapters on Intellectual Property matters, in the US and elsewhere:

Trade marks - invaluable guidelines if you are bringing/launching branded product/services in the US and elsewhere. Patents - If you are an innovator/inventor, unlock your ideas and turn them into profitable reality. This book describes the invaluable steps from concept to applying for a patent.

Connect with ExecVisa

Website: www.execvisa.com

Like us on Facebook: www.facebook.com/execvisa

Smashwords Author Profile: https://www.smashwords.com/profile/view/execvisa

Other books by ExecVisa are listed in the final pages of this book.

ExecVisa™

HERE'S HOW YOU GO ABOUT OBTAINING MANY TYPES OF VISA THAT ALLOW YOU TO WORK OR DO BUSINESS LEGALLY IN USA

8 ways to work or do business
legally in USA
6 ways to stay in USA permanently
(Green Card eligibility - unfamiliar to you)

SAFE PASSAGE TO USA

This is an easy to read and understand guide. Here is what's needed to secure a US visa to meet your needs. It tells you what you require to know and have for discussion with your immigration lawyer.

This saves you a great amount of your time and your money. It cuts down on expensive legal fees and speeds up the process. The book is wide-ranging without being exhaustive. It supplies you with invaluable guidelines.

BONUS CHAPTERS - Intellectual Property in the US and elsewhere.
Trade marks - Invaluable guidelines if you are bringing/launching branded product/services in the US and elsewhere.
Patents - If you are an innovator/inventor, unlock your ideas and turn them into profitable reality. This book describes the steps from concept to applying for a patent.

Execvisa

ExecVisa™ 亞洲人

如果您是亞洲人，在这里您将了解到如何获取使您能够在美国合法工作或开展生意的诸多签证类型

在美国合法工作或开展生意的 **8** 种方式
在美国永久居留的 **6** 种方式（您对此并不熟悉）绿卡

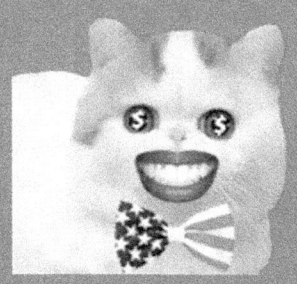

这是一本易于阅读和理解的指南。这是取得美国签证的所需事宜，以满足您的需求。您可以从这里得知您与您的移民律师进行讨论时所需了解和掌握的内容。这为您节省了大量的时间和金钱，它替您省去昂贵的法律费用，加快了整个进程，本书并非面面俱到，但是涉猎极为广泛。它为您提供了极其宝贵的指导。

附送章节：美国及其他地方的知识产权

商标 - 如果您在美国引入/推出品牌产品/服务，这将是极为宝贵的指南。

专利 - 如果您是一位革新者/发明家，解锁您的创意，将其转变成为有利可图的实体。本书描述了从概念到申请专利在内的一系列极为有用的步骤。

ExecVisa™ (Português)

COMO OBTER OS DIFERENTES TIPOS DE VISTO QUE LHE PERMITAM TRABALHAR OU FAZER NEGÓCIOS NOS EUA

8 formas de trabalhar ou fazer negócios legalmente nos EUA

6 formas de permanecer nos EUA permanentemente (desconhecidas para si) Green Card

Este é um guia de fácil compreensão. Aqui você encontra tudo sobre como obter um visto que satisfaça as suas necessidades. Tudo que você precisa de saber e discutir com o seu advogado de imigração.

Poupa-lhe tempo e dinheiro. Corta grande parte de custos legais desnecessários e acelera o processo. O livro é completo sem ser exaustivo. Fornece-lhe orientações indispensáveis.

CAPÍTULOS BONUS: Propriedade intelectual nos EUA e em outras partes. **Marcas registadas** – Orientações valiosas para quem pretende trazer ou montar produtos/serviços e marcas para os EUA. **Patentes** – Se é um inventor/inovador, liberte suas ideias e torne-as uma realidade rentável. Este livro descreve os passos desde a idealização do conceito até ao pedido de patente.

Execvisa

ExecVisa™ (Español)

CÓMO SE DEBE HACER PARA OBTENER LOS DIFERENTES TIPOS DE VISA QUE LE PERMITEN TRABAJAR O HACER NEGOCIOS EN ESTADOS UNIDOS

8 maneras de trabajar o hacer negocios legalmente en los Estados Unidos

6 maneras (desconocidas para usted) para mantenerse en los Estados Unidos de forma permanente – Green Card

El libro es una herramienta fácil de leer y entender. En él se explican los pasos necesarios para la obtención de una visa en los Estados Unidos, de acuerdo con las necesidades de los inmigrantes. Si usted es un inmigrante, el libro le explica lo que tiene que saber y tener al momento de discutir con su abogado de inmigración.

Este libro guía ha sido publicado en diferentes idiomas (en versión impresa y como libros electrónicos). Esto le ahorra una gran cantidad de tiempo y dinero. Se reducen gastos legales costosos y acelera el proceso. El libro posee un gran alcance sin llegar a ser exhaustivo. El libro le proporciona directrices invaluables.

CAPÍTULOS ÚTILES - Propiedad Intelectual en los EE.UU y en cualquier otra parte
Marcas - directrices invaluables si usted está trayendo / lanzando marcas de productos / servicios en los Estados Unidos.
Patentes - Si usted es un innovador / inventor, abra sus ideas y conviértalas en realidad. Este libro describe los pasos primordiales en cuanto a la aplicación de patentes.

Execvisa

ExecVisa™ (Indians)

IF YOU ARE INDIAN, HERE'S HOW YOU GO ABOUT OBTAINING MANY TYPES OF VISA THAT ALLOW YOU TO WORK OR DO BUSINESS LEGALLY IN USA

8 ways to work or do business legally in USA

6 ways to stay in USA permanently (Green Card eligibility - unfamiliar to you)

SAFE PASSAGE TO USA

This is an easy to read and understand guide. Here is what's needed to secure a US visa to meet your needs. It tells you what you require to know and have for discussion with your immigration lawyer.

This saves you a great amount of your time and your money. It cuts down on expensive legal fees and speeds up the process. The book is wide-ranging without being exhaustive. It supplies you with invaluable guidelines.

BONUS CHAPTERS - Intellectual Property in the US and elsewhere.
Trade marks - Invaluable guidelines if you are bringing/launching branded product/services in the US and elsewhere.
Patents – If you are an innovator/inventor, unlock your ideas and turn them into profitable reality. This book describes the steps from concept to applying for a patent.

Execvisa

IMMIGRATION CHARITY E-BOOK

THE INVALUABLE GUIDE

This is an invaluable guide for social entrepreneurs and non-profit religious, charitable, social service, or similar organizations. It is specifically written for those who wish to start and/or operate an immigration-law non-profit in USA. This guide is devised by ExecVisa

www.ingramcontent.com/pod-product-compliance
Lightning Source LLC
Chambersburg PA
CBHW071834200526
45169CB00018B/1500